What's so Bad about Hell?

Book #4 in the Little Book Series

Kent Philpott

EVP

What's So Bad about Hell?

Earthen Vessel Media, LLC
San Rafael, CA 94903
www.evpbooks.com

ISBN: 978-1-946794-14-7 print
ISBN: 978-1-946794-15-4 EPUB

All quotes contained in the "Hellacious Quotes" section
starting on page 42 were found at
https://www.azquotes.com on 11/15/2018.

Contents

Preface

Is hell good or bad? My suspicion is that some will love it, at least at first, while others will hate it.

Others are certain they are going there and hope it is not as bad as some say.

On the other hand, there will be some who definitely do *not* want to go to heaven. Going to heaven is a thought that frightens them.

Some fret and fret that they might go to hell, because they know they ought to.

Others are confident they will not go there and are grateful for that.

Wherever you are at, dear reader, maybe this Little Book will be of interest to you.

Chapter One

You'll be with your friends!

A word from your personal spirit guide:

All those annoying Christian types are nowhere to be seen. Gone. And good riddance. For this, you have me to thank.

Somehow, the Bible thumpers made you feel uncomfortable, irritable, even angry. They could never get it that everyone would be fine if they just did good deeds like protecting the environment and working to relieve oppression around the world. All they wanted to do was condemn people who disagreed with them. Rule makers parading their commandments around, making you feel guilty. "Screw guilt" was your motto.

Now you are surrounded by comrades, fellow travelers, good folk who know how to accept others without reservation. You are one in spirit and with the spirits.

You may have noticed, however, that you seem to be alone. Yes, there are hordes of others nearby, and you sort of sense this, but there is a darkness that is thick and heavy. You can almost hear the rustling; perhaps droning is a better word. You are alone but not alone at the same time. It is *virtual* aloneness.

You wonder how long the darkness will last. Don't ask me, because there is no way of knowing. It may last forever. It would not be unusual for such a fear to creep up on you. Thick darkness will make you think you are going mad. You cannot see anyone or talk to anyone; you're just alone. It has only been a little while or seems that way, but you can't help wondering what sort of place this is.

And will it ever end?

A word from your host:

You have arrived at your final destination. I have carefully managed your journey, beginning from day one.

Your parents were already on my side, so it was easy, really. You were baptized as an infant, you were taught the basics in your youth, became a member of your parents' church, and that was that. We like to say that you were "inoculated."

Yes, you attended one of those places on the special days, but that was pretty much it. When asked, you would say you were a Christian, but you did not know very much of anything about the Bible or what Christianity was all about. Thankfully! And you never really questioned much of anything. You simply did what you wanted.

There were times when you had conversations with religious bigots who talked about their weird ideas, but you managed to dodge their deceptive testimony. And no, you would not read any of the stuff they gave you and absolutely refused to attend any church meeting with them. I was with you all the way on this, constantly providing you with more exciting things to do than sing old hymns and listen to hour-long meaningless sermons.

You got married in a church, yes, but the guy with the robes and phony smile was my guy, and you never heard a word that might have alerted you to what you are now enjoying. Your wife was not interested in religious things, only spiritual things, and I am the most spiritual of them all. We had fellowship then right from the beginning. You were thoroughly insulated.

Your friends tended to be friends with me, so you were protected from any attempts to look at things differently. You enjoyed what I had to offer, though that did get you into some trouble with authorities a time or two. Still, you never gave up, and here you are. I say, well done!

Personal thoughts:

I had no idea of any of this. Neither did any of my friends, except for the kid who lived next door. Larry was his name. He went away to college, said he found

Jesus, and wanted to tell me all about it.

We chatted a few times about what he was discovering in his Bible. I mentioned to him that I had a copy of *The Satanic Bible*, written by Anton LaVey, a big deal in San Francisco during the hippie days. I thought the devil was cool and far more fun than the unbelievable characters he was talking about. Larry did mention the devil a time or two, called him a liar and a murderer. That made me mad.

One day he pressed me to come to church with him. That was it, the end of our relationship. At times I recalled one or two things he said, but I got skilled at blocking it out. Now I wish I had listened.

My hope in my later years of life was that it would all just end. Death had to be nothingness, but not this. If I only had known.

Is it too late for me? This being alone in the dark is getting to me. I thought there would be fire in hell, so this can't be hell. There is nowhere to go and nothing to do. This is unbearable. Maybe there is an ending to it all, and this is just a kind of testing, a sentence handed down by a judge, like a five to twenty-year lockup. Maybe that is it. Try as I might, I doubt it. This seems to be what I have from now on.

Or, maybe I am in what the Catholics call purgatory. Yes, maybe I will be punished for what it is that God is pissed about, then I will get out of here.

Chapter Two

No one will bother you from heaven.

_____

A word from your personal spirit guide:

Never fear, if you had friends in heaven, they will not be able to trouble you. Including your friend Larry. There is a huge and impassable gulf between you and the poor folk in heaven.

Likely none of *your* friends would be in heaven anyway. This is something we did for you. Any of the enemy who even got close to you we got rid of. You were so clever; you could see them coming.

It was easy to spot the really egregious ones; they wanted to prevent you from enjoying yourself. How tiresome to hear the "thou shalt nots." And what hypocrites, too. They thought they were so good, but you knew better.

A word from your host:

I hear you are spending serious time with your guide, developing a special personal relationship. You two can get even tighter now that the real work is complete and we have succeeded in securing your place here forever, so get used to it; here you are! And the best part is that you two will never be separated; you are its assignment. Think of it—you were guided almost from the time you were born. There was always the danger you might run into some of the enemy, but praise me, your guide is truly watching out for you.

Personal thoughts:

I got into some real trouble complaining about this ever-present darkness. Okay, right, I must try not to complain and moan. Looks like I must learn to keep everything inside.

Were those enemies, as they are called here, actual enemies? A torturing thought goes through my mind now, that maybe they really weren't as bad as I used to think. I'm thinking of Larry right now. But wait. He's the one who made me feel guilty, even rebellious, he and some of those other church goers told me they loved me, but that only made me sick. Yeah, I'm glad to be free of them now.

Chapter Three

"Better to laugh with the sinners than cry with the saints."

A word from your personal spirit guide:

What a fantastic lyric from Billy Joel. There it is, right-on all the way. Just think—you would have been crying with the saints if you had ended up in heaven. Instead, and thanks to me, you are laughing with the sinners. You ought to be grateful.

Saints. What a sickening name for the holier-than-thou types. Never having any fun, worried about something all the time. But since I kept close tabs on a few of them, I have a reliable suspicion they were sinning in their minds. Their thoughts were on evil all the time, but they tried to deceive you. You did not fall for it, and I congratulate you on that. Again, well done.

A word from your host:

Just checking in. I have to make sure my guides are doing their job. You might not know it, but there are levels in my realm. Your guide knows it well and knows that things could go south for it, if it's not careful.

And you, too. Do you think there is not more ahead for you? So far you have had it easy. Just getting adjusted, so to speak. Soon you will be scheduled for what really happens here. Full disclosure (only in the fine print) is what I am known for. You will find out why you are here, and I have to tell you that you will not be laughing with the sinners. Sorry! There is no laughter here; there is only pain, dreadful pain, and crying.

Since you are made in the image of XXX and loved by XXX, I and my hordes hate you with an inexpressible hatred. Now you know. You have nearly completed the introductory phase that all newbies experience. Get ready; more is coming.

To be completely clear, you have landed in hell—yes, that place you laughed about with your friends so often. "Go to hell," you liked to say, and you did not know you were speaking truth.

Don't think anything will ever change. You are with me and in this place forever and ever. Amen.

Personal thoughts:

Now I know for sure. If I could kill myself I would and right now. Knowing the truth is not helping. There is not a damn thing I can do about it. How I wish I could go back. I even miss Larry.

I was blinded, completely blinded, and I thought I was so superior to those church-going, so-called friends of mine. Why did I dislike them so much? What did they do to me? Why did I feel so uncomfortable around them? Why could I not have just listened a little? What harm would it have done me to go to a Bible study or a church service with them? What an idiot I am.

Now it is forever too late.

Chapter Four

You will be conscious 24/7.

A word from your personal spirit guide:

A correction is necessary right away. There is no time here in hell—no past, present, or future. It is all now and all the time. You are here for eternity, and eternity never ends.

Think of it. There is no death, no ending. You are in eternal death. Just want you to know, in case you had any hope that this wonderful experience you are having will end.

No complaining. I gave you what you wanted. Think of all the good times you had in your fun life. Wow, you did some really wicked stuff. I know, since I was right there. More than that, I did some cute little tricks to keep you going. A few times, your wonderful deeds landed you in real trouble, but I comforted you, opened doors for you, and spurred you on. Aren't you glad?

Just want you to know that I hate and despise you, and my job is to make you as miserable as I can. This is my job, and I love it.

A word from your host:

I understand that your basic instructions are complete now. Your trustworthy guide filled me in.

Now you know that everything is motivated by fear and hatred. I am the king here, and this is who I am. I hate you and you hate me. I am Lucifer, the Day Star. Have you not heard of me? I am even mentioned in that horrid book XXX came up with. How I hate it!

It is too late for this to help you, so I will quote to you what XXX said about me:

> How you have fallen from heaven,
> O Day Star, son of Dawn!
> How you are cut down to the ground,
> You who laid the nations low!
> You said in your heart,
> "I will ascend to heaven; above the stars of God;
> I will set my throne on high;
> I will sit on the mount of assembly
> In the far reaches of the north;
> I will ascend above the heights of the clouds;
> I will make myself like the Most High."
> But you are brought down to Sheol,
> To the far reaches of the pit.

(Isaiah 14:12–15)

Now you know. I did not ascend, I was sent out and descended into this hell. I was cast out, cast into Sheol, also known as Hades and Hell and Gehenna. This place was made for me, all for me and my angels, and this is my kingdom, my everlasting abode. I love it, but I hate all that is made in the image of XXX.

You are here because you are mine and not XXX's. You are a dirty rotten sinner, and XXX will have nothing to do with you. I will rule over you and all in my domain, tormenting you all forever. Yes, you will live forever, since XXX raised to immortality the just and the unjust. Yes, you will want to kill yourself, but you cannot.

I have you, and no one can take you from me. Is this not a comforting word?

Personal thoughts:

I want to die, just die. That is what all who rejected Christ hope for—to die. This is what we believed, that the universe had a shelf life, as we all do, and then it ends. We thought it would all be gone, so eat, drink, and be merry.

Was I really merry? I suppose I had some fun, usually at the expense of someone else, and I was proud of it. A real man, a risk taker and fun lover, I took what I wanted.

I was sure death would set me free. But eternal life in heaven? No, no proof of it, nothing at all. Just have faith, just believe—Larry told me so. But I would have none of it. Now I know why my guide and host hate the enemy so very much. Looks like this is all I have now—hate.

Chapter Five

You will have all your old memories.

A word from your personal spirit guide:

Yes, you will be able to remember everything, especially now that your mind is alert and you are sober. Gone are the times when you could numb yourself out and run from the pain of your living. Forever sober, something you could never achieve before. Congratulations.

Your memory completely intact, you can think back on the good old days. Why do you get to do this, you wonder. Simple, really. The memories only bring you greater grief.

What you enjoyed before, you will never enjoy again. I love this—a memory being an instrument of torture. Indeed, the giver of despair am I.

A word from your host:

Have you been thinking about your life on the planet? Good, your guide is doing its job. Just checking in again. How do you like it? You hate it, right? Wish you could turn it off, right? Forget it, you are completely damned.

Dream away. Remember old Larry? He's not long for the planet. Cancer it is, eating away. Do you think your old buddy will show up here? I'd love to have a crack at him, but damn it all, I lost him to the chief enemy. He is the only one of your crowd who escaped our net.

Personal thoughts:

There is nothing to say. I have no hope of ever having a single pleasant second. Why didn't someone warn me?

Larry did, he told me about the Light, this Jesus, who chased the darkness away. That must be why the thick darkness is like a wet blanket thrown over me. A complete absence of light of any kind.

Chapter Six

You won't have to be holy or be with holy people.

A word from your personal spirit guide:

If there is one thing wonderful about hell, it is that you will not have to hang out with holy people, those sickly-sweet do-gooders. Not one from the holier-than-thou crowd will be here. So there you are, something even an idiot can appreciate.

Of course, even if one such should be found in our abode, you would never know it, due to the heavy darkness that permeates all. You are all each alone, alone forever. The only company you will keep will be with the utterly unholy, mainly me.

Not only will there be no holy saints around, you don't have to be holy yourself. You delighted in unholiness in your lifetime, so now you can have at it. You now abide in the unholy of unholies. You can be as evil as you want to be, but ha! Now you will be by yourself, so you will have to figure out how you can be unholy and evil without anyone to take advantage of.

A word from your host:

Have you sunk into the lowest you can go yet? Too early, no doubt. Still, it is usual that you are plunged into despair with the realization you can't get out of here.

Forget about people still alive who might offer a prayer, light a candle, pay for a mass to be said for you—that was all just a gimmick I cooked up long ago. I call it "false assurance," and millions went for it and still do. It was one of my best moves.

No, you will never get out. Aren't you glad you will never have to suffer at the hands of the holy again?

Personal thoughts

Why did I reject those Christians I knew back in high school, especially Larry? If I had it to do over, I would at least listen and try to figure out what he was saying. I can only think that there was something I feared, feelings that bothered me—something, but I am not sure what. I'm such an idiot, which my guide likes to say.

Now I can't contact anyone, can't go back—no phone calls here, nothing but aloneness and darkness. I would settle for some fire, yeah, even hell fire. I thought there would be fire and light. No light, no heat, just me and the spirit guide.

What about the demons? I only know of one and its boss. Not much, and I am going out of my mind.

Chapter Seven

You will live forever.

A word from your personal spirit guide:

Consider the gift you have been given: eternal life. Even XXX's book says it: the resurrection of the just and the unjust.[1] You are in the category of the unjust, thus yours is, as Daniel said, "shame and everlasting contempt," or as the son of XXX said, "the resurrection of judgment," and as the ex-rabbi Paul put it, "the resurrection of the unjust."

One way or the other you will live forever; it all has to do with destination. You bought your ticket, waited at the station, and boarded the train to hell. Look at it that way if you will, but here you are.

Indeed, you will never get over it. Forever you will be tormented by the fact that this is your final destination. Get used to it. Torment is your companion.

A word from your host:

Are you settling in now? Hope so. You have to get rid of any notion that your situation will ever change. It is

---

1 Check the following biblical references on this point: Daniel 12:2; John 5:29; and Acts 24:15.

eternal, it is permanent, and this is perhaps the greatest of all horrors you now get to experience.

You got tricked. That little pip-squeak Larry was easy to compromise. You found out quickly he was a hypocrite, as all of XXX's chumps are. And he got resurrected, too, but you will not find him here.

Personal thoughts:

I am utterly shocked that I ended up in hell. There were plenty of guys who were far worse than me. Some of my friends went far beyond anything I would ever have done.

To the best of my knowledge, I never *really* hurt anyone, at least as far as I was concerned. Pretty much I was your normal everyday guy, taking advantage of situations for my own gain, but who didn't?

I considered myself a fair-minded person, a loyal American, and helped others when I could, so why me and why here? Just because I didn't go for the religious stuff, does that make me a bad person? Larry liked me, I had friends, got along with my parents and my brothers, worked hard at my job, made decent money, raised a family. . . Come on, just a regular middle-class guy. Doesn't all that count for something?

Apparently not.

Chapter Eight

You won't have to sing any hymns.

A word from your personal spirit guide:

There are a number of things you won't ever have to do again. Let's see now, you won't have to eat or drink anything, or go to sleep or take a nap, wear clothes or go on vacations. You won't have to go to work, put up with stupid family members or neighbors, have to go shopping or work out at the gym. No television, no movies, no sports, no theater, no books, no newspapers, really nothing to see or do. This is our specialty—you won't be doing anything at all.

Best of all you won't have to sing any of those miserable hymns. You won't be hearing any hymns either, because there is no sound to be heard except from the boss and me; well, there is the moaning and groaning of the hordes trapped here, but even that will be faint and ill-defined.

Actually, you do not even need any of your senses except hearing. You will hear your guides and Master, that's all. Experience has shown that you will want to stop your ears from hearing us, but you will not be able to do it.

A word from your host:

We do not need to hear your praises here, since we already know what you are thinking. Even speaking is over. All that which humans do while on the planet, you will never do again. Yes, you hear me, but that is the end of it. You know that I am the god of this world. I rule—the ultimate strong man!

I like it dark and empty, nothing but consciousness. The best of all evils.

Personal thoughts:

Once Larry tried get me to go to his church to hear some Christian band. If I had, my friends would have made me feel like a jerk. I told him some lie. Wish I hadn't.

Here I am in hell, and I don't want to be. I'd like to hear some music. Never thought of it until just now—no more music, no television, no movies, no plays, nothing again, ever again.

I am not sure I can even make a sound. I cannot hear myself. I only have thoughts. How crazy! My existence is demons, the devil, and my own mind.

Chapter Nine

You will obey your master.

A word from your personal spirit guide:

Let me make this short and simple: as yet you are not aware that things can get worse for you. To be very plain, you are merely at the first level of hell; there are others. To avoid them, you must obey our great ruler without any dissent, nothing but complete compliance will be accepted.

A word from your host:

I will accept nothing from you but total obedience and worship. All else is blasphemy, the worst of the worst. Worship is more than mere obedience but includes it. And don't think you are off the hook because you can't speak. All your thoughts are known to us, so get used to thinking your praise and adoration of me, which I must have, since I am the god of this world, this death, this hell.

One other little exciting point: you were wrong all along. You didn't get it at all. You completely had the wrong view of the world, which is not surprising, since

I have my propaganda folks working on it full time. Advertising pays.

Personal thoughts:

At least I know what I am to do. This is my total meaning and purpose for eternity. I will worship all that is evil and horrid.

How did it come to this? Probably this thought has been recorded, and what it will cost me, I don't know. But all I can do is think—impossible not to.

Was I different from the rest of my friends? No, there were at least two others that were far greater sinners than me. I didn't hate Larry; he was one of my few actual friends, maybe my only real friend. He never gave up on me; I rejected him. Now I live with this.

Chapter Ten

You won't have to love or even be kind to anyone ever again.

A word from your personal spirit guide:

No one loved you ever. That so-called friend Larry kept telling you were loved by the arch-enemy, but he lied. He tried to trick you into going to church with him. Those hypocrites just lie, lie, lie.

How could you be loved? You were only interested in yourself. You used people to get what you wanted. You never cared for them in any way at all. You deserve what you are getting, so never forget it.

A word from your host:

I overheard what your guide said to you, and let me tell you it is spot on. You have been and always will be only a self-lover.

You will not love me, either. You will hate me with a level of hatred unimaginable. Love here is truly hate. Utter hate will completely fill you, leaving room for nothing else.

Personal thoughts:

Guess it must be true; I can even feel it happening to me. There are yet the memories I have of good feelings toward by parents, at least when I was little. That changed over time to the point I wanted to break away from them. Later I pretty much ignored them.

I did not feel loved. I don't know if I loved anybody else. I wanted, I craved, I starved for lots of stuff, but I think I missed love all together. How did this happen to me? I got cheated, and it makes me angry to the point I hate everything and everybody.

Chapter Eleven

Is hell really that bad?

A word from your personal spirit guide:

Once you get used to it, you will discover that hell is really not that bad. After a while you will accept your eternal lot and flow with it. But not completely, since you will have your conscious memories, which is part of our torment strategy.

Do you see this is not merely a kind of holding pen, this is a place of weeping and gnashing of teeth, which is an old fashioned way of describing the horrors of your new abode.

A word from your host:

One last reminder to you before your spirit guide takes 100% control. You are never leaving here. You are locked in the ultimate prison. This is all you have or ever will have.

There is no one here to feel sorry for you. You are here to be punished. That book Larry spoke to you about was right, but my fallen angels where right there to prevent you from taking anything seriously. Blind darkness, thicker than tar, and you didn't have any idea.

I detect a question that you have. You wonder why all of this is. Let me explain it to you. You are made in the image of XXX, meaning that you could love XXX and XXX love you. I hate XXX and XXX banished me to these nether regions. But for a short time as we count it, eons as you humans do, I have waged a war against all those loved by XXX. I despise XXX and I despise you.

I'm the winner in the numbers game, because he rescues only a few, while I get the lion's share. You are only one of billions. Yes, XXX got the babies and the kids and the mentally impaired, and a bunch of others, but I got mine, and I am after millions more.

How long before the final judgment comes is unknown. Therefore, I am doubling down with my murdering ways, pitting tribe against tribe, nation against nation. Yes, I love it—wars and rumors of wars.

I am the great divider. My goal is to have everyone hating and murdering one another. It is becoming easier and easier to do this. On the scale, I am the big winner. Think of it this way: I have already lost all that can be lost but I am taking as many with me as possible. You are mine, and I am yours. And that is that.

Personal thoughts:

I hate the devil. Since I do not have the capacity to love, at least I can hate. This is the reward of hell. I hate everybody and everything. Each moment I will give myself to hate.

Most of all, I hate myself.

Chapter Twelve

What must I do to be saved?

You are invited to believe in Jesus Christ. You are called to repent of your sin and become a follower of Jesus.

More than that, you are *commanded* to believe in Jesus, to trust that His death on the cross and the shedding of His blood was for the purpose of you being forgiven of your sin and given the gift of eternal life.

Peter proclaimed in the first Christian sermon ever preached, "Repent therefore, and turn again, that your sins may be blotted out" (Acts 3:19).

It is your own sin that will send you to an eternal hell. Do you want to keep to your sinful ways and thereby earn the awful reward of spending eternity in a devil's hell?

No, this is not what you want. Read what one of the greatest of preachers, Charles H. Spurgeon, proclaimed to his London Church on August 14, 1861:

> Oh! the thought above all thought the most deadly, I am lost, lost, lost! And this is the horror of horrors: I have caused myself to be lost; I have put from me the gospel of Christ; I have

destroyed myself. . . .

Oh, my hearers, Will any man choose for himself to be lost? Will he count himself unworthy of eternal life, and put in from him? If you will be damned, you must do it yourselves. Your blood be on your own heads. Go down to the pit if you deliberately choose to do so, but this know, that Christ was preached to you, and you would not have him; you were invited to come to him, but you turned your backs on him; you chose for yourselves your own eternal destruction! God grant that you may repent of such a choice, for Christ's sake. Amen.

C. H. Spurgeon, a Baptist who believed firmly in the doctrines of grace, meaning election and predestination as we find in Romans 8:30, "And those he predestined he also called, and those who he called he also justified, and those whom he justified he also glorified," also knew of the invitation, the command to believe in the Savior, Jesus Christ.

I invite you reader right now to carefully read the following passage from the Gospel of John, chapter six.

Verse 35: Jesus said to them, "I am the bread of life; whoever comes to me, shall not hunger, and whoever believes in me shall never thirst.

Verse 36: "But I said to you that you have seen

34

me and yet do not believe.

Verse 37: "All that the Father gives me will come to me, and whoever comes to me I will never cast out.

Verse 38: "For I have come down from heaven, not to do my own will but the will of him who sent me.

Verse 39: "And this is the will of him who sent me, that I should lose nothing of all that he has given me, but raise it up on the last day.

Verse 40: "For this is the will of my Father; that everyone who looks on the Son and believes in him should have eternal life, and I will raise him up on the last day."

Will you believe that Jesus died on the cross to save you? Will you now repent of your sin and trust Jesus to save you?

And once you now see Jesus as your Lord and Savior, will you follow His command to be baptized? Here are the very words of Jesus on this point:

All authority in heaven and on earth has been given to me. Go, therefore, and make disciples of all nations, baptizing them in the name of the Father and of the Son and of the Holy Spirit, teaching them to observe all that I have commanded you. And behold,

I am with you always, to the end of the age.
Matthew 28:18–20

Then take it an important step further: Find a church, a brick and mortar church, with a real pastor and a congregation, one where Jesus is proclaimed and the Bible is read and preached, and get involved. You have only just begun the great adventure, and you now will have the experience of growing up into being a mature Christian.

If you are having difficulty with this, visit the website of the church where I am pastor, the Miller Avenue Baptist Church in Mill Valley, California. That site is: www.milleravenuechurch.org.

We will do our best to get you connected with a local church.

Postscript

Some of you will think I am a literalist with my rather bleak take on hell. Darkness! Aloneness! Forever! Torment! Memories! Yes, this is bleak at minimum.

Not all Christian theologians view hell as I do. However, I present it as I find it in the Bible. A critic or two might say I soft-pedal hell, since I do not mention the possibility of flames, worms that do not die, demons with pitch-forks, and other well-known images or models. Maybe I deserve the evaluation.

C.S. Lewis, in *The Great Divorce*, pictures hell as just the ongoing nature of life on the planet as we know it, yet without the presence of a loving God or any love at all. That would be hellish enough.

Other Christians think that at our death or at the Second Coming of Christ, and following the Great Judgment, all who do not go to heaven will be annihilated. I see this as an easy out and unbiblical. We must provide full disclosure.

Let me explain why I wrote this Little Book on hell.

First, I accept Jesus' statements as to the reality of hell. That He believed in hell is unquestionable per my reading of the Gospels.

Second, theologically speaking, since sin can never be in the presence of God, sin must be put away. The core story of Scripture is that God utterly put away the sin of His chosen ones through the death of His Son, Jesus Christ, on the cross. The Father placed all our sin upon the Son. All of our sin, from day one to the last day of our lives, was placed firmly upon Jesus. His shed blood cleanses the sinner of all sin. Those, then, who have not been washed in the blood of Christ cannot be in His presence, and since both the just and the unjust are raised to eternal existence, there is hell.

Third, my own personal experience persuades me. As a psychology major in college, I was certain the Bible's accounts of demon possession were nothing more than misguided first century psychology. I knew better, I thought.

However, during my years ministering with the hippies in the San Francisco's Haight-Ashbury District, I found out differently. I detail this in other books (see especially *Deliver us From Evil: How Jesus Casts Out Demons Today*).

My master's thesis, *A Manual of Demonology and the Occult*, published by Zondervan Publishing House in 1973, instigated many hundreds of people to come to me for what we call "deliverance ministry." From the beginning of the 1970s to the 1980s, I engaged with many others in the casting out of demons. During that period, I wrote *The Deliverance Book* with R. L. Hymers, Jr., which we wrote in an effort to keep people from travelling to where I lived in San Rafael, California, to receive ministry.

It was overwhelming. At one point, there were fourteen two-person teams trained to deal with the surge of dear folks needing freedom from the demonic. I say this to indicate my level of knowledge about the subject. Even to this day, this ministry continues but without the numbers coming for help as we saw during the 1970s.

My point is simple: many hundreds of times I have heard demons crying out as they are about to be cast out, pleading not to be sent to hell.

Yes, you might want to read that sentence again.

Jesus encountered the same situation in the story of the casting out of a legion of demons found in Mark 5:1–20. A deranged man, likely suffering from mental illness caused by demon possession, approached Jesus. He had a "legion" of demons that desperately hoped Jesus would cast them into a herd of pigs. They wanted to be "in flesh."

As strange as it might seem, I cannot forget the many times demons began shrieking and screaming when they were ordered to go to hell. Readers, you may think this is absolutely crazy, but it is not. The demonic spirits often began by loudly demanding that they not to be sent into "the pit of hell," then finally pleading weakly as they could see their fate.

Early on, I had a hard time with this. For hours following a "deliverance session" I would wonder if it all really happened. At times a number of us would be gathered together, and we would discuss our ministry. There were events where others from various parts of the country arrived, and we all had the same stories to tell. These were neither delusions nor hallucinations.

As time wore on, I had to face the fact that not only were there actual unclean spirits, or demons, but that hell was indeed a reality. I sincerely wish it were not so. The Scripture's testimony, coupled with that of many others down through the centuries added to my own direct and personal experiences to prevent me from denying it. To do so would be a terrible deception.

How can I deny the facts?

But if I could, I would like to believe that death is the end of it all—annihilation. A few times over the years I have been accused of sending people to an everlasting hell, which is likely an emotional reaction, as I have no power or authority to do any such thing. No one creates reality but God.

My only choice is to see what the Scripture says and attempt to present that. My appeal is that the reader should examine the material and arrive at his or her own conclusions.

Index of References to Hell in the Bible

Some Christians take the biblical images of hell as literal, and others do not. There is a considerable history to the terms used to describe that *place* called Sheol, hell, hades, or Gehenna. There are scores of books on the subject. The details are interesting and sobering, but the bottom line is that hell is real, and all those who are not safe in Christ at His return or their dying will certainly be elsewhere than in the presence of God in what we call heaven.

Certainly, Satan and his demons, those fallen angels, will be separated out and will be in that *place* we call hell. Indeed, that which is unholy would far rather be in hell than in heaven.

No Christian delights in hell or is happy that people will be sentenced to it. My mother and brother were not followers of Jesus, not even close, and it is with sadness and heaviness of heart that I have written this piece. While I wish it were not so, it is so. The plain truth must be told.

So then, this Little Book is written for those who are not safe in Christ, those who are yet dead in their trespasses and sins. Here is full disclosure, which is not that common these days, since few wish to offend non-Christians. Real followers of Jesus will not shrink from presenting the whole of the truth and would rather please the Savior than give false comfort to those who are perishing.

There are about 150 references to hell in the whole of the Bible.

Following are references to hell, or *sheol*, or hades in the Hebrew Bible, our Old Testament.

Sheol is a transliteration from the Hebrew word for the world of the dead or the unseen state. There are thirty-two passages where the word is found. These are:

Genesis 37:35; Deuteronomy 32:22; 2 Samuel 22:6; Job 11:8; 26:6; Psalms 9:17; 16:10; 18:5; 55:15; 86:13; 116:3; 139:8; Proverbs 5:5; 7:27; 9:18; 15:11; 15:25; 23:14; 27:20; Isaiah 5:14; 14:9; 14:15; 28:15; 57:9; 38:10; Ezekiel 31:16; 31:17; 32:21; 32:27; Amos 9:2; Jonah 2:2; and Habakkuk 2:5.

From the most ancient portions of the Hebrew Bible, Genesis and Deuteronomy, we have references to a place of the dead, who are in a conscious state of existence. This *sheol* is no heaven; rather it is a place of torment exactly as Jesus and other writers of the Greek Bible so describe and warn about.

Also note that Islam's scriptures also speak a great deal about hell and hell fire. Other world religions also speak of a place of torment that follows death.

Following are some common references for hell found in the New Testament only.

Matthew 3:7 From John the Baptist: "the wrath to come"

Matthew 5:22 From Jesus, Sermon on the Mount: "the hell of fire"

Matthew 5:27 Also "whole body being thrown into hell"

Matthew 7:13 Jesus speaks of the way that "leads to destruction"

Matthew 8:5–13 Jesus speaks of "outer darkness" and "weeping and gnashing of teeth"

Matthew 10:28 Jesus says, "rather fear him who can destroy both soul and body in hell"

Matthew 13:42 Jesus speaks of "that place where there will be weeping and gnashing of teeth"

Matthew 13:49 Jesus says, "The angels will come out and separate the evil from the righteous, and throw them into the furnace of fire: there men will weep and gnash their teeth. . ."

Matthew 18:8–9 "And if your hand or your foot causes you to sin, cut it off and throw it away. It is better for you to enter life crippled or lame than with two hands or two feet to be thrown into the eternal fire. And if your eye causes you to sin, tear it out and throw it away. It is better for you to enter life with one eye than with two eyes to be thrown into the hell of fire."

Matthew 22:13 Jesus speaks of outer darkness and weeping and gnashing of teeth.

Matthew 23:33 Jesus says, "You serpents, you brood of vipers, how are you to escape being sentenced to hell?"

Matthew 25:46 "and they will go away into eternal punishment but the righteous into eternal life.

John 5:28-29 "Do not marvel at this, for an hour is coming when all who are in the tombs will hear his voice and come out, those who have done good to the resurrection of life, and those who have done evil to the resurrection of judgment."

Romans 2:5 Paul speaks of the "day of wrath."

2 Peter 3:7 Peter speaks of "the day of judgment and destruction of the ungodly."

Jude 6–7 Jude speaks of "eternal chains, nether gloom, and judgment of the great Day. And punishment of eternal fire . . ."

Jude 13 "for whom the gloom of utter darkness has been reserved forever"

Rev. 4:9–11 "And another angel, a third, followed

them, saying with a loud voice, "If anyone worships the beast and its image, and receives a mark on his forehead or on his hand, he also shall drink the wine of God's wrath, poured unmixed into the cup of his anger, and he shall be tormented with fire and brimstone in the presence of the holy angels and in the presence of the lamb. And the smoke of their Torment goes up forever and ever; and they have no rest, day or night, these worshipers of the beast and his image, and whoever receives the mark of its name."

Rev. 16:10 "Speaking of the beast, or Satan, we have: "The fifth angel poured out his bowl on the throne of the beast, and its kingdom was plunged into darkness. People gnawed their tongues in anguish and cursed the God of heaven for their pain and sores."

Rev. 19:20 These two were thrown alive into the lake of fire that burns with brimstone.

Rev. 20:10 ". . . the devil who had deceived them was thrown into the lake of fire and brimstone where the beast and the false prophet were, and they will be tormented day and night forever and ever."

Rev. 21:8 "But as for the cowardly, the faithless, the detestable, as for murderers, the sexually immoral, sorcerers, idolaters, and all liars, their portion shall be in the lake that burns with fire and brimstone, which is the second death."

Hellacious Quotes*

Augustine
"Hell was made for the inquisitive."

Thomas Aquinas
"I answer that, Even, as in the bliss in heaven there will be most perfect charity, so in the damned there will be the most perfect hate."

Richard Baxter
"In hell, sinners shall forever lay all the blame on their own wills. Hell is a rational torment by conscience."

Alistair Begg
"Would anyone choose Hell over Heaven? YES! Why? Pride. They don't want to go in the only way you can go in, on your knees. They don't want to admit they are a failure, that their life is a mess."

William Booth
"Most Christians would like to send their recruits to Bible college for five years. I would like to send them to hell for five minutes. That would do more than anything else to prepare them for a lifetime of compassionate ministry."

John Calvin
"When a certain shameless fellow mockingly asked a pious old man what God had done before the creation

of the world the latter aptly countered that he had been building hell for the curious."

D.A. Carson
"Hell is not filled with people who are deeply sorry for their sins. It is filled with people who for all eternity still shake their puny fist in the face of God Almighty."

G.K. Chesterton
"The men of the clique live together because they have the same kind of soul, and their narrowness is a narrowness of spiritual coherence and contentment, like that which exists in hell . . ."

Richard Dawkins
"The fear of Hell is a very powerful motivation."

John Donne
"Solitude is a torment which is not threatened in hell itself."

Jonathan Edwards
"Almost every natural man that hears of hell flatters himself that he shall escape it."

John Flavel
"Oh sirs, deal with sin as sin, and speak of heaven and hell as they are, and not as if you were in jest."

Pope Francis
"Let us never give in to pessimism, to that bitterness that the devil offers us every day. Do not give in to

pessimism and discouragement. We have the firm certainty that the Holy Spirit gives the Church with His mighty breath, the courage to persevere and also to seek new methods of evangelization, to bring the Gospel to the ends of the earth."

Billy Graham
"God will never send anybody to hell. If man goes to hell, he goes by his own free choice."

Christopher Hitchens
"There's no Hell mentioned in the Old Testament. The punishment of the dead is not specified there. It's only with gentle Jesus, meek and mild, that the idea of eternal torture for minor transgressions is introduced."

Timothy Keller
"It is because of the doctrine of judgment and hell that Jesus' proclamations of grace and love are so astounding."

C. S. Lewis
"The descent to hell is easy and those who begin by worshipping power, soon worship evil."

Abraham Lincoln
"I had been told I was on the road to hell, but I had no idea it was just a mile down the road with a dome on it."

Max Lucado
"First, God does not send people to hell. He simply

honors their choice. Hell is the ultimate expression of God's high regard for the dignity of man. He has never forced us to choose Him, even when that means we would choose Hell."

Martin Luther

"I admit that I deserve death and hell, what of it? For I know One who suffered and made satisfaction on my behalf. His name is Jesus Christ, Son of God, and where He is there I shall be also!"

George MacDonald

"I would not favour a fiction to keep a whole world out of hell. The hell that a lie would keep any man out of is doubtless the very best place for him to go to. It is truth... that saves the world."

J. Vernon McGee

"Don't say that a loving God is going to send you to hell— He's not. The thing that's going to send you to hell is that you're a sinner and you don't want to admit it."

Albert Mohler

"Hell will be filled with people who were avidly committed to Christian values."

John Milton

"Nor aught availed him now to have built in heaven high towers; nor did he scrape by all his engines, but was headlong sent with his industrious crew to build in hell."

John Owen

"Satan's greatest success is in making people think they have plenty of time before they die to consider their eternal welfare."

J. I. Packer

"Scripture sees hell as self-chosen. . . Hell appears as God's gesture of respect for human choice. All receive what they actually chose. Either to be with God forever, worshipping Him, or without God forever, worshipping themselves."

John Piper

"The greatest cause in the world is joyfully rescuing people from hell, meeting their earthly needs, making them glad in God, and doing it with a kind, serious pleasure that makes Christ look like the Treasure he is."

Adrian Rogers

"I believe that a great number of people are going to die and go to hell because they're counting on their religiosity in the church instead of their relationship with Jesus to get them to heaven. They give lip service to repentance and faith, but they've never been born again."

Leonard Ravenhill

"Let us never give in to pessimism, to that bitterness that the devil offers us every day. Do not give in to pessimism and discouragement. We have the firm certainty that the Holy Spirit gives the Church with His mighty breath, the courage to persevere and also to seek new methods of evangelization, to bring the Gospel to the ends of the earth."

J. C. Ryle

"Beware of manufacturing a God of your own: a God who is all mercy, but not just; a God who is all love, but not holy; a God who has a heaven for everybody, but a hell for none; a God who can allow good and bad to be side by side in time, but will make no distinction between good and bad in eternity. Such a God is an idol of your own, as truly an idol as any snake or crocodile in an Egyptian temple. The hands of your own fancy and sentimentality have made him. He is not the God of the Bible, and beside the God of the Bible there is no God at all."

Dorothy L. Sayers

"The doctrine of hell is not "mediaeval priest craft" for frightening people into giving money to the church: it is Christ's deliberate judgment on sin.... We cannot repudiate hell without altogether repudiating Christ.

R. C. Sproul

"Like Muslims we assume that God will judge us 'on balance.' If our good deeds outweigh our bad deeds, we will arrive safely in heaven. But, alas, if our evil deeds outweigh our good ones, we will suffer the wrath of God in hell. We may be "marred" by sin but in no wise devastated by it. We still have the ability to balance our sins with our own righteousness. This is the most monstrous lie of all."

Charles Spurgeon
"Morality may keep you out of jail, but it takes the blood of Jesus Christ to keep you out of hell."

John Steinbeck
"My imagination will get me a passport to hell one day."

Hunter S. Thompson
"If there is in fact, a heaven and a hell, all we know for sure is that hell will be a viciously overcrowded version of Phoenix."

A. W. Tozer
"The purpose of God isn't to save us from Hell. The purpose of God is to make us like Christ."

Mark Twain
"Now is the accepted time to make your regular annual good resolutions. Next week you can begin paving hell with them as usual."

Rick Warren
"I do believe in hell. Jesus spoke more about hell than heaven - I trust him as the authority, not you, me or anybody else. If hell is not real, then Jesus was a liar and God has a lot of explaining to do on His justice and things like that."

John Wesley

"Consider that all these torments of body and soul are without intermission. Be their suffering ever so extreme, be their pain ever so intense, there is no possibility of their fainting away, no, not for one moment ... They are all eye, all ear, all sense. Every instant of their duration it may be said of their whole frame that they are 'Trembling alive all o'er, and smart and agonize at every pore.' And of this duration there is no end ... Neither the pain of the body nor of soul is any nearer an end than it was millions of ages ago."

George Whitfield

"If one evil thought, if one evil word, if one evil action, deserves eternal damnation, how many hells, my friends, do every one of us deserve, whose whole lives have been one continued rebellion against God!"

David Wilkerson

"God hates the LUKEWARM GOSPEL OF HALF-TRUTHS that is now spreading over the Globe. This gospel says, 'Just believe in Jesus and you'll be Saved. There's nothing more to it.' It ignores the Whole Counsel of God, which speaks of Repenting from former Sins, of Taking up your Cross, of being conformed to the Image of Christ by the refining work of the Holy Spirit. It is totally silent about the Reality of Hell and an After-Death Judgment."

Ravi Zacharias

"The Biblical world-view is the only one that accepts the reality of evil and suffering while giving both the cause and the purpose, while offering God-given strength and sustenance in the midst of it."

*The URL for the site used to obtain the above quotes is: https://www.azquotes.com

www.ingramcontent.com/pod-product-compliance
Lightning Source LLC
Chambersburg PA
CBHW071739020426
42331CB00008B/2093